OUR FIRST GRAMMAR

OUR FIRST GRAMMAR

ELLIS A. DAVIDSON

GYAN

Published by

Gyan Publishing House
5, Ansari Road
Daryaganj, New Delhi-110002
Phone: 011-47034999, 9811692060
E-mail: books@gyanbooks.com

Distribution Network
gyanbooks.com
India, USA, Canada, UK, Australia

ISBN: 978-93-7414-153-3 (PB)

First Published, 1870

2nd Impression 2026

Printed at: Gyan Press, Delhi.

OUR FIRST GRAMMAR
Author: ELLIS A. DAVIDSON

OUR FIRST GRAMMAR.

OUR

FIRST GRAMMAR

With 100 *Exercises for Home Work, and Questions for Examination.*

BY

ELLIS A. DAVIDSON,

AUTHOR OF "LINEAR DRAWING," "PROJECTION," ETC. ETC.

LONDON:

CASSELL, PETTER, AND GALPIN;

AND 596, BROADWAY, NEW YORK.

INTRODUCTION.

THIS little book is offered to Parents and Teachers in the hope that by its means some few of the difficulties experienced in teaching grammar may be removed.

The object kept in view in its compilation has been to make the study pleasant to children; this has been attempted by the introduction of simple stories and poems as exercises, and it is hoped that by this method the little pupils may become interested in what they are learning.

Parsing, as such, has been avoided, the children being merely called on to "sort out" the words, all further detail being deferred until the groundwork shall have been laid, and the pupil shall have advanced to the absolute study of grammar, to which this is only an introduction.

The exercises follow each section, so that an opportunity is afforded for testing whether the children have really comprehended the lessons given, or for varying them if required.

I have an intense objection to what is termed "learning in play," which weakens instead of strengthening the mental powers. Still, there is no reason why all the lessons should not be adapted to the character of children, nor why, in the early stages, the instruction should not be made as amusing and pleasant as the subject will admit.

Nature has made children bright and joyous, and if it be right to promote the proper development of their physical powers, it must be equally correct to render their mental culture free and happy. Thus to observe a child crying over a lesson which is too difficult for it to comprehend, is as abnormal a state of things as to see another who is unable to bowl a hoop which is too heavy for it to raise.

A feeling of real affection for our young charges, and of sympathy with their joys and sorrows, has guided me in writing this little book, and I earnestly hope that the effort herein made may prove successful.

ELLIS A. DAVIDSON.

February, 1870.

OUR
FIRST GRAMMAR.

TO LITTLE BOYS AND GIRLS.

In this little book you are going to learn how to speak in a plain and clear manner, so that any one hearing you may know exactly what you mean.

If you have a box of bricks you will know that some of them are long and others short—some straight and others arched—some are blocks and others are pillars.

Now, in playing with these bricks, you have to put each in its proper place, if you want your house to look pretty or to stand safely.

Each piece will have its purpose, and if you do not put it in its proper place your building will be ugly, or will tumble down.

Now, it is just the same in speaking. The sentences we use are made up of nine kinds of words, and if we do not put these in their proper places, the letter we may write, or the tale we may tell, will only be a jumble of words mixed up anyhow, and would no more sound like good English, than the heap of bricks thrown out of the box would look like a pretty house.

I will give you a slight notion of the sorts of words used. They are called the "nine parts of speech:"—

1. Nouns—which are the names of things we can see or think of; as, **Horse, Honesty.**
2. Ar-ti cles. Little words put before some nouns. There are only two of them; **a** and **the.**
3. Ad-jec-tives tell us something about nouns; as, "**good** boys."
4. Pro-nouns are words used instead of nouns; as, in the sentence, "The man went away, but **he** did not come back again," **he** is a pronoun.

5. Verbs tell that something is done, exists, or suffers; as, "I **am**," "I **jump**," "I **feel**."
6. Adverbs tell **how** a thing is done; as, "John writes **well**." **Well** is an adverb.
7. Pre-po-sitions show the relation of words or ideas to others; as, "John is **at** school." **At** is a preposition.
8. Con-junc-tions join words together; as, "You **and** I." The word **and** is a conjunction.
9. Inter-jec-tions are used to show surprise or pain; as, "**Oh!** look." **Oh!** is an interjection.

As you read further in this little book, and work the lessons in it, you will be taught more about these parts of speech, and the proper way to use them. You will find some nice little tales, showing how words are put together, and if you attend to all that is said, you will soon learn to **use right words in their right places.**

NOUNS.

When we look about us we see a great many things.

If we are in the school-room we see **desks, benches, tables, books, maps, slates**; and if we could only look into each other's **pockets,** we should most likely see **apples, tops, nuts,** and **marbles.**

Now, all these are names of things, and **all words which are names are called Nouns.**

Here are some more nouns. Write them down that you may not forget them :—

Exercise 1.

Ant	Goat	Mole	Tub
Bat	Hand	Nail	Urn
Cat	Ice	Owl	Van
Duck	Jar	Pin	Wig
Egg	Key	Rat	Yew
Fan	Lock	Stork	Zone

These are all very easy names, because they are such little words that you can say them at once, and they are therefore called words of one syl-la-ble.

EXERCISE 2.

Write down twenty more such little words; and to be sure that they are **nouns**, say to yourself, before you write any one of them, "**Is it the name of a thing?**" and if it is not, do not put it down. To make my meaning more plain, let us suppose you think the word "mew" is a noun. Well, if you ask yourself, "Is it the name of anything?" you would at once see that it is not. But the **cat** mews, and **cat is** the name of a thing; so the word **cat** is a **noun.**

Now, whilst we are learning these little words, I will tell you something about the letters of which they are spelt.

Of course, you know your A B C, or you could not read even these words; but you must be told that only very little children call the letters A B C. Children who are clever enough to begin to learn grammar call them the **Al-pha-bet.**

Well, then, amongst the letters of the al-pha-bet

there are five which are so very useful that **we cannot spell a word** without some of them. They are A, E, I, O, U, and you will see that the names of them are such simple sounds that you could not spell them with any other letters. These five letters, A, E, I, O, U, are called **vowels.**

In the list of nouns which I have given you, I have printed all the vowels in black letters, and you will see that if you were to take these away, you could not make up a word of the letters which would be left. Take away the A from Ant and **nt** remains. If you take the **a** out of Bat, B-t would not spell anything. Take the **a** out of Can, and you will leave only C-n; and if you take the **u** out of Duck, only Dck remains; and if you were to take the **e** away from the next noun, you would quite spoil the **Egg**, for the gg, which would be left, would not even be the shell.

When we have taken the five vowels away from the Alphabet, twenty-one letters, called **con-so-nants**, are left, these are—

b c d f g h j k l m n p q r s t v w x y z

Consonants are of no use at all unless we get some vowels to help them to make up words; in fact, if you were to write down their names, you would have to spell them with the aid of a vowel —b-e be, c-e ce, d-e de, e-f ef; and this, you will find, would be the case with all of them.

When w and y stand at the beginning of a word or syllable, they are called con-so-nants, but in every other place they are vowels.

Exercise 3.

Write down twenty words, and put a mark like this — under every vowel.

Having given you this short lesson about letters, we can now return to nouns.

Exercise 4.

Fable.—The Dog who went out to Sup.

A man made a great feast, and his dog Tray said to Gyp, who was a great friend of his, "Come and sup with us to-night. Eight o'clock is the time; but if you are there an hour too soon you will find there is much to be done." Gyp lay in the sun awhile to wink and wait. He thought of fish, flesh, and fowl, tripe and toast, and made a feast in his heart that made a bill of fare for a king. At length the time came, and he set off to the cook's room, where he found all hands hard at work. Gyp went with a skulk—now here, now there—gave a peep at this dish, and smelt at that, and with a wag of his tail, as much as to say, "O! rare! what a feast I have in store!" His wag of the tail brought the eyes of the cook on him, and he said, "How, now? What's this I spy? A cur! Who let him in? A nice sort of guest to be sure! I shall soon pack you off. The cook then brought poor Gyp to view, and threw him out at the back door.

There's oft a slip 'twixt cup and lip.

Copy this fable, and put a mark like this —— under each noun in it.

The noun **dog** is called **singular**, because only **one dog** is meant.

The noun **dogs** is called **plural**, because a **number** are spoken of.

There are several ways of altering words which are singular, so as to make them plural. One way is to add a letter **s** to the singular, thus :—

Singular	Cat	Plural	Cats
,,	Toy	,,	Toys
,,	Bat	,,	Bats
,,	Girl	,,	Girls
,,	Rat	,,	Rats
,,	Cart	,,	Carts
,,	Lamb	,,	Lambs
,,	Hat	,,	Hats
,,	Cap	,,	Caps
,,	Cup	,,	Cups
,,	Stick	,,	Sticks
,,	Book	,,	Books
,,	Plant	,,	Plants

Singular	Pen	Plural	Pens
,,	Plum	,,	Plums
,,	Nut	,,	Nuts

Exercise 5.

Write down twenty nouns, and in another column placed like mine, write the plurals of them, but your nouns must only require the letter **s** to be added to them to make them mean plural instead of singular. Sometimes we have to add **es** to the singular to turn it into the plural, as in the word dish. We do not, if we want to speak of more than one dish, say dishs, but dish**es**, and I will now give you a little tale in which you will find the singular words turned into the plural in the two ways I have told you of, and you must observe that I have put one line thus — under the single s which I have added, and two lines thus = under the **es**. The little story is called

HOME FOR THE HOLIDAYS.

Many years ago, some boys were going home from school to spend their holidays. Each boy had packed up his box, and when they were all brought down into the passage there was a whole row of boxes. They wished before they went away to say "good-bye" to their master's lady, who had been so very kind to them all the half-year, but they had been in the playground having a last turn on the giant's stride, or a game of leap-frog, and their coats were dusty, so they each took a brush and began rubbing the other down, like horses being groomed, and all the brushes at work together soon made the cloak room very cloudy. They did not stop long there, but knocking at the parlour door, soon heard a voice say, "Come in." On the table they saw a large cake; and I suppose you know that all boys are fond of cakes; then there was a glass of milk for each boy—a whole row of glasses—so they had a nice lunch before they started.

The school was not near a railway; for there were not then as many railways as there are now, so they were going home by the coach, and very pleasant it is to ride on coaches, for you see the country around and enjoy the fresh air.

Just as they were leaving the village, little Tommy Jones took out his watch; *he* said it was to see the time, but Johnny Brown said it was only to show the watch, which had just been given to him. However, they all looked at their watches, and at the clock in the tower of the church, and as they drove along they looked at the clocks in all the churches they passed.

By-and-by a fox rushed across the road, his long bushy tail trailing behind him; whilst at a distance they saw the hunters, in their red coats, spurring on their horses and hallooing to the hounds, and all the boys agreed that it is very cruel to hunt the poor foxes to death just for pleasure.

Well, all the little boys got safely to their homes, each gave a kiss to his mamma, and many kisses to his sisters. Some of them, instead of spending the whole of their pocket-money on cakes, balls, and tops, had saved some of it, and had bought brooches, sashes, or work-boxes for their dear ones at home; and their sisters loved them all the more, not for the mere value of the presents, but because they showed that their brothers thought of them when they were away.

Now, telling nice little stories is all very well when we have nothing else to do, but we have some work on hand; but before we go on I should like to be quite sure that you have learnt something by the tale you have read, so I will ask you to think over the way in which the **names** of the **things** are made to mean the plural instead of the singular, and then to work this lesson for me:—

Exercise 6.

Write down all the words in the tale which are turned into the plural by only adding **s** to the singular. Put these in a column—that is, write each name **under** the last one instead of at the side of it; then write down all the words to which we have added **es.**

When you have done this put down ten more words like those in the one column, and ten more like those in the other.

Some nouns which end in **o** are turned into the plural by **es,** without the word being sounded as if another syllable had been added. Thus we have

Singular	Hero	Plural	Heroes
"	Negro	"	Negroes
"	Potato	"	Potatoes

and, of course, you know that these words are pronounced as if they were written, Herose, Negrose, Potatose.

Now, if you were to hear a boy say, "I have two **pen-knifes,**" I am quite sure you would laugh, and you would whisper to one of your friends, "I wonder where that boy has been to school." But before we find fault with other people, we ought to be quite sure that we know why they are wrong; so I will tell you the rule for such words as knife. It is, that **most nouns which end in f or fe change their last letters into ves.** I will give you a few of such words, and you will then be able to find some more like them:—

Singular	Life	Plural	Lives
„	Knife	„	Knives
„	Sheaf	„	Sheaves
„	Leaf	„	Leaves
„	Calf	„	Calves
„	Loaf	„	Loaves

Then again, if you wanted to write to a boy to tell him not to be cruel to animals, you would, perhaps, say, "It is a very wicked thing to hurt the poor flies," you would not spell this word **flys**; and I will tell you why: it is because **nouns ending in y with a consonant before it, change the y into ies to form the plural.** Thus we have:—

Singular	Fly	Plural	Flies
„	Duty	„	Duties
„	Baby	„	Babies
„	Pantry	„	Pantries
„	Lady	„	Ladies
„	Cherry	„	Cherries

Exercise 7.

Write two sentences, using some words in which the plural is formed by changing **f** or **fe** into **ves**, and two others in which the **y** is altered to **ies.**

Exercise 8.

Try to write a little tale, so as to use some of the words you have been learning about. I will just give you an outline of a story, and then you can use your own words, and tell it in any way you like.

You might begin by telling us why **boys** and **girls** like to go into their mothers' **pantries,** and why it is wicked to kill the **flies,** which you will most likely find buzzing around the **pots** of jam.

Then tell us about going out into the fields; how we may see some men digging up the potatoes, others cutting down the corn with bent, hook-like knives called sickles, and setting it up in sheaves, whilst ladies are walking on the banks of the river, and the babies are having their airing in their nurses' arms.

You need not use these exact words, but any others which are turned from singular into plural by either of the rules you have learnt.

Then there are some nouns which I dare say you will think very troublesome little words, because they will not agree with either of the rules. To turn them into plural we have to alter, sometimes one letter and sometimes another, until the whole word seems changed. I will give you a few of these nouns:—

Singular	Goose	Plural	Geese
„	Mouse	„	Mice
„	Man	„	Men
„	Child	„	Children

Singular	Tooth	Plural	Teeth
,,	Foot	,,	Feet
,,	Ox	,,	Oxen
,,	Penny	,,	Pence or pennies

EXERCISE 9.

Read this fable, and make a list of all the nouns in it; then against those which are singular write the plural, and against such as are plural write the singular:—

THE MAN, HIS SON, AND HIS ASS.

A man and his son drove their ass to market to sell him. They had not gone far when one of a group of girls, who stood round a well, said, with a laugh, "Look at those two fools; they let their ass walk at his ease while they trudge on foot by his side." The man heard this, and set his son on the beast. They had not gone more than half a mile when they came up to some old men, who sat on a bank. "There," said one of them, "that just proves what I say: now-a-days the young take no care of the old. See, that young rogue rides while the old man has to walk by his side. Get down, and let your sire rest his limbs." At this, the man made his son jump off the ass that he might ride him. Thus they went on for a space, when they met three kind dames, each with a child on her arm. "Why, you old sloth," said one of them, "what a shame to sit at ease while that poor slight lad can scarce keep pace by the side of you." The man then took up his son on the croup of the ass by his side, and so they rode till they got near the town. "Pray, good friend," said a young man who met them, "is that ass your own?" "Yes," said he. "One would not have thought so by the way you load him. Why, it seems to me more fit that you two should take him to the fair than that he should take you." "Well, be it so," said the old man; "we can but try." So they got off, and made fast the legs of the ass to a pole, which they took hold of, one at each end. And so they went on their way till they came to a bridge. This was a rare sight, and so the boys and girls thought, for they ran in crowds to laugh at the fun; till the ass, which took fright at the noise, gave a kick, and broke the cords which bound him, so he fell into the stream and sank. The old man made the best of his way home, and said, "If we try to please all, we please none, and may lose all we have."

GENDER.

But it is not enough to know that nouns are either singular or plural, we must show whether they are male, female, or neither—and this is called describing their **gender**.

There are two genders. The—

Mas-cu-line—which means living things that are male; as, a man.

Fem-i-nine—which means living things that are female; as, a woman.

Things which are not alive, and therefore are neither male nor female, are called **Neuter**; as, a stone.

There are three ways of showing whether the noun is masculine or feminine.

The first of these is by giving to the female a name quite different from that of the male. You will see what I mean in these words:—

Male	Man	**Female**	Woman
,,	Boy	,,	Girl
,,	Cock	,,	Hen
,,	Ram	,,	Ewe
,,	Stag	,,	Hind
,,	Buck	,,	Doe

Exercise 10.

Write the feminine of each of the following nouns:—

Boar	Dog	Drake	Gander

and the masculine of the next six nouns :—

Sow	Cow	Woman
Mare	Ewe	Duck

The second manner of forming the feminine of nouns is by adding **ess** to the masculine ; as—

Male Lion, **Female** Lioness

Sometimes we alter the end of the masculine name before we add ess. Thus, we do not say, male—tiger ; female—tiger-ess ; but we spell the word **tigress.**

Exercise 11.

Write twelve nouns which are feminine, and twelve which are masculine.

The third method of showing whether the noun is masculine or feminine is the easiest of all. It is by placing another word in front of it, which tells all about it. Thus :—

Man-servant	**Maid**-servant
He-ass	**She**-ass
Male-child	**Female**-child
He-goat	**She**-goat

This is so very easy that you will not be required to work an exercise upon it, so I will now speak of nouns called **Neuter**, which, as I have already told you, means that they are the names of **things**, not of **animals.**

Now, I dare say you know quite as many nouns which are neuter as I do. There is your **hoop,** your **bat,** your **ball,** your **apples,** your **buns,** your **books,** and thousands of other things; so you will find it very easy to work the next lesson.

EXERCISE 12.

Write down in one column twenty nouns which are neuter, and of the **singular** number, and in another column write the plurals of them; in this way:—

Singular	Cart	**Plural**	Carts
„	Knife	„	Knives
„	House	„	Houses

Neuter, then, means **neither** male nor female; but there are some words which are names of persons or animals, but which still do not say plainly whether males or females are meant. Thus, if I say, "I have seen some **children** playing," or, "I have passed through a **crowd** of **people**," "I love my **parents**," "I am fond of **animals**," I am mentioning several nouns, but I do not state exactly whether they are males or females; but you are quite certain they are not dead **things**, like sticks or stones.

Then, just for once in a way, think, and ask yourself, "Were these children **boys** or **girls**?" Then you will remember that **children** may be **either** or **both**.

A crowd of people." Were all these people, who were looking at some fine sight in the street, **men**, or were they all **women?**" Well, you will soon remember that they were **both.** Then you will think of your dear **parents,** and you will see that here again we mean **both.**

As to animals, you know that cocks and hens, billy-goats and nanny-goats, the tom-cat, with his big head and saucy face, and his quiet, sleek wife, are all **animals.** Therefore, the word does not mean any single male or female, but **both.**

Well, then, all the nouns which mean **both** masculine and feminine, or either, are called the **Common gender.**

Exercise 13.

Sort out the following nouns, and place them in columns according to their gender :—

Cup, Duke, Governess, Cattle, Friends, Emperor, Chair, Widow, Soldier, Servant, Box, Cousin, Ball, Captain, Neighbour, Slave, Poultry, Pupil,

Teacher, House, Dog, Cow, Coach, Table, Bird, Sow, Man, King, Queen, Ram, Girl, Fish, Garden, Organ, Boy, Sailor, Nurse, Candle, Cat, Book, Cock, Picture, Mare.

And then, for

EXERCISE 14,

Write down six nouns that are of the feminine gender, six that are masculine, twelve that are neuter, and six that are of the common gender.

Now I will give you a nice little poem, which I am sure you will like.

MORNING.*

1.

The little lambs skip on the lawn;
  The bees hum round the flowers;
The cock has crow'd the morning's dawn;
  The owl has left the towers;

* From "Poems for Children," by E. A. Davidson.

2.

The horse has gone to draw the cart;
  The ass his load to carry;
The workmen to their labour start,
  Then should we children tarry?

3.

No, let us rise; but ere we play,
  To God our praises render,
For guarding us by night and day,
  With love so great and tender.

4.

But then we must not idle be,
  Amidst so many beauties;
For all things God has made, we see,
  Have purposes and duties.

Exercise 15.

Write out the first two verses of this little poem, and then learn them by heart.

EXERCISE 16.

Write out the last two verses, and learn them by heart; then write down the gender and number of all the nouns in the whole poem.

Still, I have not finished all I have to tell you about nouns. It is not enough to know their number and their gender, but we must know their **case.**

Case tells you whether the noun is the name of the person **doing something**, or of a person to whom something is **being done**, or of a person to whom something **belongs**; but you must know case refers to all nouns, whether they are the names of persons or of things.

Now let me show you what I mean in a little sentence. Suppose you know a boy named John, whose father has given him a nice little pony. You go out and meet one of your schoolfellows, and, wishing to tell him a piece of news, you say, "**John** rides a pony."

Well, "John" and "pony" are both nouns, you know; but John is riding, so **he is doing something**; whilst the pony is **being ridden**—that is, **something is being done to it.**

John is therefore said to be in the **Nom-i-native** case, because John is the agent, or **person acting.**

Pony is said to be in the **Objective** case, because it is the object which is **acted upon.**

But if you say—

"The **pony** carries **John,**"

then the **pony** is the principal thing you are speaking of, for the **pony** is doing something **for John,** and therefore in this sentence **pony** is in the **nominative** case, and **John** is in the **objective.**

You can always find out which is the nominative case, if you ask yourself the question, "Who?" or "What?" Thus, if you ask, "**Who** rides a pony?" the answer will be, "**John**"—so, John is the nominative.

Again, you can find out which is the objective, by asking yourself the question, "What?" or

"Whom?" So that if you say, "**What** does John ride?" the answer will be, "A **pony**"— so that **pony** is the objective.

Now, before I tell you any more about cases, I must see if you have understood what I have said thus far; so you may work

EXERCISE 17.

The woodman felled the tree.
The tree struck the woodman.
The dog gnaws the bone.
Bones please dogs.
The ship struck a rock.
Tommy teased pussy.
Pussy scratched Tommy.

Copy these sentences; rule two short lines thus ═══ under the nominative, and one thus ——— under the objective, in each sentence, as I have done, in the following examples:—

He went to school.

School improves boys.

The master loves the boys.

The boys love the master.

Exercise 18.

Write twelve sentences with nouns in the nominative and objective cases in them. Rule the double and single lines under them, to show which you mean for nominative and which for objective, as in the last exercise.

But there is another "case," called the "Possessive." I dare say you will at once know what this means; and I fancy I hear you whispering to the boy next you, "Oh, that means having something belonging to us"—and so it does.

Let us return to our friend John. If his father gave him a pony, the pony was his property. So that when you saw him cantering along, you might have said, "That is **John's** pony;" then the noun "John's" would be in the possessive case.

You will see that to turn the noun "John" into the possessive case, I have put a comma, called an a-pos-tro-phe, above the line, and then a letter s.

Exercise 19.

Copy the following examples, and then write ten more yourself:—

The woodman's axe is sharp.

The dog's bone.

A ship's anchor.

The pussy's claws.

Tommy's hoop.

When the nouns have been turned into the plural number by the addition of s, then we only put an apostrophe after it, and not another s. Thus, supposing your sister Mary lends you her ball, and, as would be most likely, you lose it;

you want to borrow another; you are ashamed to ask your sister Jane for her ball, so you write on your slate to your friend Jones, and you say: "My dear Jones, I have lost my sister's ball, will you be so very good as to lend me yours?"

But Jones will **not** be so *very* good, he thinks that perhaps his ball might just take a fancy to go and look for your sister's, so he buttons up his pockets, and is too busy at his lessons to attend to your request.

Then, when you get home, your sister Jane, who (like most of our sisters) is very kind, comes out and offers you her ball, and she says, "Now mind, Dicky, that you are very careful of it;" and you show your care by trying if you can throw it over the house, and you manage it, for the ball goes nearly, nay quite, out of sight, and you comfort yourself by saying, "I did not mean to do it." But anyhow you say, "As I have lost the balls which both my sisters lent me, I must open my money-box and buy them new ones, for I have no right to be careless of my sisters' property.

So that you see where the noun sisters only meant the plural number you simply added s, but when it means plural and possessive as well, you do not add another s and say sisters's, but only put an apostrophe after the word.

Exercise 2C.

Copy the following examples, put one line under the nouns which are plural only, and two under those which are plural and in the possessive case as well :—

Boys will be boys, but they should not soil other boys' books.

The parrots were tumbling head over heels in a very funny manner, until they began to peck at each other, and you know parrots' beaks are very strong.

The moment I held out a bone, the twenty dogs began to wag their tails; twenty dogs' tails all wagging at the same time was a queer sight to look at.

Exercise 21.

Copy the following sentences, and put the apostrophe in its right place in each :—

Fathers stick.	Workmens tools.	Lions manes.
Boys books.	Dogs skins.	Birds wings.
Charles book.	Williams slate.	Babys shoes.
Girls dresses.	Ladies bonnets.	Englands glory.

Exercise 22.

Write ten short sentences something like the last, each showing a noun in the singular number and the possessive case.

Exercise 23.

Write ten short sentences, each showing a noun in the plural number and the possessive case.

But even now I have something more to tell you about nouns, and that is, that they are divided into two sorts, called **common** and **proper**, but the difference is so very plain that you will understand it the moment you are told.

Exercise 24.

Copy the following rule, so that you may remember it:—

Common nouns are the names of all the common things around us, of which there may be many of the same sort, such as dog, cat, boy, girl, toy, house, and all such nouns which mean that the thing or animal you name is one belonging to many of the same sort.

Exercise 25.

Copy the following rules:—

Proper nouns are the names of particular persons or things, which belong to themselves and not to a crowd of others.

All names of **people** are **proper nouns**; for example, if I say, "**Peter** is a good boy," then **Peter** is a **proper** noun, and boy a common noun.

All names of **places** are **proper nouns**; as, **London, Paris, Denmark.**

All names of **rivers** and **mountains** are **proper nouns**; as, **Thames, Alps.**

The first letter of a proper noun must be a capital.

Exercise 26.

Copy the following sentences, and rule a double line under the proper nouns, and a single one under the common nouns:—

David loved Jonathan.

London is a fine city.

James plays the organ.

The boys saw the Queen.

Mary plucked a rose.

The Thames is a great river.

Painting is a delightful art.

Botany teaches us about plants.

England is a happy land.

Winter is a cold season.

There are many mountains in Wales.

The French are our friends.

Exercise 27.

Write six short sentences, each having a proper and a common noun in it.

Be careful to put capitals to the proper nouns.

Well, at last we are going to leave the nouns. and speak of another sort of words, called

ARTICLES.

You may be quite sure I shall not ask you to write a long list of words called articles, for there are only **two**, and these are **a** and **the.**

Now, if I were to say to you, "Fetch **a** book," you would go and get **any** book you might find on the desk; but if I were to say, "Fetch **the** book," you would know that I mean one which I had been reading, so that the word the points out **which** book I am asking you to fetch.

Again, supposing all the school-boys are in the playground, and the master wants one to help him to put some books in their places, he does not care which boy, for he knows they are all glad to be of use to him, so he says to the servant, "Send **a** boy to me," and the servant tells the first boy he meets to go to his master.

But if some naughty boy has thrown a stone and broken a window, the master calls to the monitor, "Tell **the** boy who threw the stone to come to me;" and so you will see that the meaning of **the** is different from **a**, because **the** points out exactly **which** boy is meant, whilst **a** might mean **any** boy in the whole school.

Now, I must tell you that when we tell a child the exact meaning of any word, we are said to "**define**" it, because to define means to point out,—to explain—to make clear.

For this reason **the** is called the **definite** article, because it points out the **exact** thing meant.

But **a** is called the **in**definite article, because it does **not** define which person or thing is spoken of.

A is changed into **an**, when the word which comes after it begins with a vowel, or with a letter **h** which is not sounded (an **h** which is not sounded is called a silent **h**); thus we say **a** man, but **an** owl, or **an** hour, because **owl** begins with a vowel, and **hour** begins with a silent **h**.

Exercise 28.

Copy the following nouns, and place before them the indefinite article :—

Apple	Oyster	Ox	Inkstand
Box	Foot	Harp	Bottle
Ant	Lamb	Egg	Urn

Exercise 29.

Copy the following sentences, and add either **a**, **an**, or **the**, where you think an article is wanted :—

—— sun shines on us by day, and —— moon by night.

I have —— pretty dog.

—— Queen of England.

I bowled my hoop for —— hour.

—— master of —— school gave —— boys —— holiday.

We saw —— ape and —— horse.

Of course, you will see that **a** and **an** can only belong to nouns which are in the singular number; for whether you say **a** horse or **an** hour, it is clear you only mean **one** horse or **one** hour, but the definite article, **the**, may mean either the singular or plural number; for you can say the **dog**, or the **dogs**, the **man**, or the **men**.

But it is not enough that we should know whether nouns are singular or plural, or that they are masculine, feminine, or neuter, we want to know more about them; so we use words which are called

ADJECTIVES.

Adjectives tell us the quality of nouns. Suppose you tell me that you have **a dog**, I should not be much the wiser. I should not know what sort of a creature he is; he may be **black** or **white**; he may be **large** or **small**; he may be **fierce** or **tame**; but if you were to tell me at once that he is a **pretty little black dog**, I should be better able to understand what kind of a dog you have; so all words such as, white, large, small, fierce, tame, pretty, little, and black are **adjectives.**

Adjectives, besides telling us the quality of nouns, tell us their number. Thus in the sentences—" The dog has **four** legs, but the parrot has only **two**, " the words **four** and **two** are adjectives, because they tell us exactly how many legs the dog and the parrot have.

Exercise 30.

The following words are adjectives; copy them,

and place an article before them and a noun after them.

Example.

A good boy	— brown —	— ugly —
— little —	— deep —	— brave —
— sweet —	— old —	— clean —
— dark —	— warm —	— long —

Exercise 31.

Copy the following sentences, and rule a line thus —— under each of the adjectives.

A high wall.
A green tree.
A tall boy.
An idle man.
The black cat.
Three pounds ten shillings.
A nice cake.
A sweet apple.
A sharp knife.
An empty box.
The tame rabbit.
A new book.

Exercise 32.

Copy the following nouns, and put adjectives before them.

—— baby	—— house	—— coat
—— pony	—— ladder	—— mountain
—— lesson	—— chair	—— bird
—— river	—— girl	—— toy
—— garden	—— flower	—— fish
—— mouse	—— kitten	—— picture

Now I must tell you, that although adjectives show us the quality of the nouns, we have to alter them a little, so that they may point out whether two or three things are exactly the same, or, if not, how they differ from each other.

Three boys, William, Henry, and Richard, came out of school one after-noon, and William said, "I have a **long** lesson to learn—nearly a page."

"Oh!" said Henry, "mine is nearly two pages, so it is **longer** than yours."

"But mine is three pages, so it is the **longest**," cried Richard.

So you see all the lessons were **long**, but still

they were not equally so, and the difference is shown by comparing them with each other.

Do you know what I mean when I say *comparing them?* Well, I will tell you.

When William, Henry, and Richard reached home, their mother poured out their tea, but as she knew that they did not all like their tea equally sweet, she put one piece of sugar into the first cup, two into another, and three into the last. She was called away, and little William, who was rather a sweet tooth, was in a puzzle as to which he should take, so he took a teaspoon and tasted each. This was **comparing** them with each other. Then he found that the one was **sweet,** the other **sweeter,** and the third the **sweetest.**

So that you see there were three sorts or **degrees** of sweetness, and these are called the **three degrees of comparison.**

The first, **Sweet,** is the plain adjective, which tells you the taste of the tea. This is called the **Positive** degree.

The second, **Sweeter,** shows that you have compared the one cup with the other, and that, however sweet the other may be, this one is sweeter. This is, therefore, called the **Comparative** degree.

The third, **Sweetest.** This shows that you have compared **all** the cups of tea, and that neither of them is as sweet as this one; and this is called the **Superlative** degree.

Most adjectives are compared by adding **er** to the Positive to form the Comparative, and **est** to form the Superlative.

Exercise 33.

Compare the following nouns, as shown in the first one:—

Positive.	*Comparative.*	*Superlative.*
Dark	Darker	Darkest
Near	———	———
High	———	———
Low	———	———
Bright	———	———

Soft	———	———
Quick	———	———
Light	———	———
Warm	———	———
Kind	———	———
Cold	———	———
Fat	———	———

Exercise 34.

Write down ten more adjectives, and compare them by adding **er** and **est.**

Adjectives of two or more syllables are generally compared by adding the words **more** and **most** to the positive. Thus :—

Positive.	*Comparative.*	*Superlative.*
Beautiful	**more** beautiful	**most** beautiful

Exercise 35.

Compare the following adjectives :—

agreeable	fortunate	curious
horrible	sensible	valuable

Write down six more adjectives, and compare them in the same way.

There are some adjectives, however, which cannot be compared in either of the methods I have told you of, but require a word quite different from the positive to form the comparative or superlative. Thus we have—

Positive.	*Comparative.*	*Superlative.*
Good	better	best

Exercise 36.

Write down the comparative and superlative of

Bad little much many

and under each write the adjective which means exactly the opposite.

Some adjectives are formed from proper nouns. Thus, a man born in **England** is an **English**-man. They should always begin with a capital letter.

Exercise 37.

Write down the following examples of adjectives which are formed from proper nouns :—

Nouns.	*Adjectives.*	*Nouns.*	*Adjectives.*
Europe	European	Holland	Dutch
Asia	Asiatic	Prussia	Prussian
Africa	African	Austria	Austrian
America	American	Italy	Italian
Australia	Australian	Canada	Canadian
Japan	Japanese	Egypt	Egyptian
Rome	Roman	Wales	Welsh

Write down the proper nouns from which the adjectives in the following sentences are taken :—

A French poodle	Irish linen
Indian corn	Chinese tea
German toys	English ships

Exercise 38.

Copy the following words, and write against them the adjectives which have exactly the opposite meaning :—

honest	clever	thick
happy	quick	empty
kind	blunt	cold
cheap	smooth	right
public	coarse	long
true	straight	thin
dark	broad	tight
open	low	wet

I will now give you a pretty little poem, called

THE LITTLE LAMB.

1.

O little lamb, how much you seem
To love your mother dear!
You frisk about her on the grass,
Without a thought of fear.

2.

No prowling wolf may enter here,
To tear your snow-white fleece,
So you may eat and drink and play
In perfect joy and peace.

3.

I saw a little child to-day,
In deepest mourning clad,
Unlike the happy frisking lamb,
No mother dear she had.

4.

For she was gone far, far above
The white clouds in the sky,
To wear a shining crown of light
And dwell with God on high.

5.

Poor orphan, we must soothe her grief
And take her home to play,
And strive by little acts of love
To wipe her tears away.

Exercise 39 (or home lesson).

Write and learn verses 1 and 2.

Exercise 40.

Write and learn verses 3, 4, and 5.

EXERCISE 41.

Write down in one column all the adjectives in this little poem, and against each write the noun which it qualifies.

PRONOUNS.

Pronouns are words used instead of nouns, so as to avoid using the same word over and over again. Thus, instead of saying, "Willie is a good boy; Willie learns Willie's lessons; Willie's master loves Willie," we use pronouns, and say, "Willie is a good boy; **he** learns **his** lessons; **his** master loves **him**."

Instead of saying, "The man is charitable; the man is useful; the man is happy," we say, "The man is charitable; he is useful; he is happy."

There are three kinds of Pronouns—

1. Personal. 2. Relative. 3. Interrogative.

Personal Pronouns are used to avoid repeating the name of a person or thing.

I is called the **first** person, because it is the person speaking, as in the sentence, "I am going out;" and as it is only one person speaking, it is called the first person singular.

We is called the first person plural, because it means more than one person speaking.

Thou and **You** are called pronouns of the **second** person, because they refer to the person or persons **to whom** we speak. Thus we say, "**Thou** art the man," "**You** are a good boy."

Thou can only be used when we are speaking to **one** person, and, therefore, it is always singular.

You is not only used when speaking to **several** persons, but also when we are speaking to **one**. It is generally used in the place of **thou**; so that instead of saying, "Thou art the man," we might say, "**You** are the man."

You is therefore the second person singular, and the second person plural as well. Thus when we say, "You are a good boy," the pronoun you is singular, but when we say, "You are good boys," it is plural.

The person **of whom** we are **speaking** is called the **third person.**

If we are speaking of a male we say **he**; if of a female, we say **she**; if of an object which is neither male nor female, we say **it.**

The plural of each of these is **they.** Thus—

"I like Charley, **he** is so kind;" or, "I like Charley and Johnny, **they** are so kind."

"Mary will not come out, **she** is busy;" or, "Mary and Jane will not come out, **they** are busy." Or,

"This apple is ripe, **it** is quite sweet;" or, "These apples are ripe, **they** are quite sweet."

I hope you have understood what I have said, but to make it still more plain, I will place the personal pronouns before you at one view.

PERSONAL PRONOUNS.

	Singular.	*Plural.*
1st person, masculine or feminine	I	We
2nd person, masculine or feminine	Thou	You or Ye
3rd person, masculine	He	They
3rd person, feminine	She	They
3rd person, neuter	It	They

Exercise 42.

I will fetch John, and we shall play.

Thou wilt be happy, because thou art good.

He works with another man, and they divide the earnings.

She teaches the girls, and they attend.

It is a pretty shell; they are plentiful on the beach.

We are going out to-day.

You are walking fast.

They were very busy.

Write out separately all the pronouns you can find in these sentences, and sort them into first, second, or third person, singular or plural, masculine, feminine, and neuter.

I have already told you about the nominative, the possessive, and the objective cases of nouns, and these belong to pronouns as well.

The following example will make this clear to you:—

First Person, Masculine or Feminine.

	Singular.	*Plural.*
Nominative Case	I	We
Possessive Case	My or Mine	Our or Ours
Objective Case	Me	Us

Exercise 43.

Write three sentences, each containing the first person in the nominative, possessive, and objective cases, either in the singular or plural number. This example will show you what you are to do:—

Example.

"**I** want **my** dog to come to **me**." You will see which is the nominative if you say, "**Who** wants the dog?" The answer is, "**I** do."

Possessive.—"Whose dog do you want?"—"**My** dog."

OBJECTIVE.—"To whom do you want the dog to come?"—"To me."

Second Person, Masculine or Feminine.

	Singular.	*Plural.*
Nominative	Thou	You or Ye
Possessive	Thy or Thine	Your or Yours
Objective	Thee	You

EXERCISE 44.

Write three sentences, one containing the second person, singular or plural, in the nominative, another in the possessive, and the last in the objective case.

Third Person Masculine.

	Singular.	*Plural.*
Nominative	He	They
Possessive	His	Their or Theirs
Objective	Him	Them

EXERCISE 45.

Write three sentences, each containing the third

person, singular or plural, in either the nominative, possessive, or objective case.

Third Person Feminine.

	Singular.	*Plural.*
Nominative	She	They
Possessive	Her or Hers	Their or Theirs
Objective	Her	Them

Exercise 46.

Write three sentences, each containing the third person feminine, singular or plural, in either the nominative, possessive, or objective case.

Third Person Neuter.

	Singular.	*Plural.*
Nominative Case	It	They
Possessive Case	Its	Their or Theirs
Objective Case	It	Them

Exercise 47.

Write three sentences, each containing the third person neuter, singular or plural, in either the nominative, possessive, or objective case.

Relative Pronouns.

Relative pronouns are those which show how the pronoun and the noun relate to each other. Thus in the sentence, "The book **which** you gave me," the word "which" is a relative pronoun, and relates to "book." Book is called the Ante-cedent, which means "going before," because it is the word which goes before the relative pronoun.

There are three relative pronouns—**who, which,** and **that.**

Who can only be used to persons, as:—

The man **who** brought the parcel.
The boy **who** likes cakes.
The girl **who** has a doll.

Which is used to animals or things, as:—

The dog **which** barks at night.
The desk **which** I locked.

That is used either with persons or things, as:—

The child **that** is sick.
The boat **that** he made.

Sometimes the word **what** is used as a relative pronoun; it means **that which.** Thus, if I say, "You know **what** I want," it means, "You know **that which** I want."

When **that** is used to point out a particular thing, it is called a **Demonstrative** pronoun; as in the sentence, "Bring me **that** book."

That refers to distant things, as "**That** tree;" and **this** to such as are near, as "**This** is the house."

Exercise 48.

Add relative pronouns in the following sentences:—

The man — did it.	The girl — sings.
The horse — was lost.	The cat — scratches.
The box — I mended.	The artist — painted it.

Exercise 49.

Write seven short sentences, each containing a relative pronoun.

In-ter-rog-a-tive Pronouns.

Interrogative pronouns are only the relative

pronouns—Who, Which, and What—used to ask questions; as—

Whose cap is this?

Which boy did this?

What noise is that?

Exercise 50.

Write nine short sentences, each containing an interrogative pronoun.

Exercise 51.

Write down the pronouns in the following sentences, and sort them into the three classes—Personal, Relative, and Interrogative.

Edward and his brother have been to see me.

Have you seen my new ball?

This book is mine, and that is yours.

She lost her dog.

Who will go with me?

He gave the letter to me.

The bird that sings so sweetly.

What a noise you make.

VERBS.

Verbs are words which tell that something is done, exists, or suffers.

Whenever you relate what has happened, or whenever you ask a question, or whenever you give a command, there must be a verb in the sentence, thus :—

I **walked** to school. (This is telling what you **did.**)

Bring your dog with you. (This is telling some one what to **do.**)

What did he **say** ? (This is **asking** what he did.)

Here you have three verbs—**Walk, Bring,** and **Say.**

Before I tell you any more about verbs, we will make sure that you really know them from other words, and the most pleasant way for you to show this is by working the following exercise.

Exercise 52.

Write down **all the verbs** you can find in the following tale:—

THE PIG AND THE DOG.

A pig and a dog were taken on board a ship. They were very good friends; they ate out of the same plate, walked about the decks together, and would lie down side by side under the bulwarks in the sun. The only thing about which they quarrelled was, where they should sleep. Toby the dog had a very nice kennel, in which he used to stretch himself on some straw, just popping his nose out at the door to see if anybody passed that way with some bones. But Piggy had nothing of the sort, and he did not see why Toby should be better housed at night than he. So every night they struggled, each trying to get first into the kennel. If the dog got in, he showed his teeth and snarled, and the pig had to look out for other lodgings. If Grunter won the battle, Toby could not turn him out, but had to go away grumbling. One evening it was very windy, the sea was running very high, and it was raining very hard. The pig was slipping and tumbling about the deck; and at length it was so unpleasant that he thought the best thing he could do was to go and secure his berth for the night, though it yet wanted a good time to dusk. But when he came to the kennel there lay Mr. Toby safely housed, for he knew just as much about the weather as the pig did. "Oh, dear—oh, dear," grunted Piggy, looking up to the black sky; but Toby did not offer to move. At last the pig seemed to give it up, and took a turn as if to see where he might find a warm corner to sleep in. Presently he went to that part of the vessel where the tin plate was lying off which they ate their meals. He took it in his mouth, and carried it to a part of the deck where the dog could see it, but some distance from the kennel; then, turning his tail towards the dog, he began to make a noise as if he was eating out of the plate. "What," thinks Toby, "has Piggy got some potatoes there?" and he pricked up his ears and looked hard towards the plate. "Champ, champ," goes the pig, and down goes his mouth to the plate again. Toby could stand this no longer. A supper, and he not there! Out he ran, and, pushing the pig on one side, put his cold nose into the *empty* plate. The pig turned tail in a moment, and before the dog knew whether there was any meat in the plate or not, he was snug in the kennel, laughing at poor Toby's folly.

Now, after such a pleasant lesson you must not mind a little hard work, so I am going to ask you to attend very carefully whilst I teach you more about verbs.

A **transitive verb** is one which tells of an action done to another person or thing. The word transitive means **passing over**, and these verbs are called transitive because the action passes over to an object. Thus—

I teach William. Here the agent—that is, the person acting or doing something—is **I.** The aot

I am doing is **teaching**; the object I am acting upon—that is, the person I am teaching, is **William.**

EXAMPLES OF TRANSITIVE VERBS.

Exercise 53.

Copy these. Rule one line under the agent, or *person doing something;* one line under the object acted upon—that is, the *person to whom something is done;* and two lines under the *verbs.*

I helped an old man.
Rabbits eat cabbage leaves.
John hurt my finger.
The hen broke her egg.
The dog bit me.
The child played a game with toys.
Columbus discovered America.
How did he hurt you?
Have you eaten your dinner?

My mother gave me a picture.

The squirrel eats nuts.

I saw Punch and Judy.

EXERCISE 54.

Write twelve other sentences, each containing a transitive verb.

When a verb tells of something being done, but does not say to whom it is done, it is called an **intransitive verb.** Intransitive means **not** passing over; and these verbs are so called because **the action does not pass over to an object.** Thus, in the sentence—

" The dog barks,"

I am telling you that the dog is doing something, but not that he is doing it **to anybody or anything,** so that in this case the word **barks** is an intransitive verb.

EXAMPLES OF INTRANSITIVE VERBS.

Exercise 55.

Copy the following sentences. Draw a line under the intransitive verbs in them.

The ship sailed.	I shall soon leave.
I slept soundly.	The parrot talks.
The sun rises.	The bird flies.
The storm passed by.	My horse fell.
The boys laughed.	The soldiers marched.
The flowers fade.	The water froze.

Exercise 56.

Write twelve sentences, each containing an intransitive verb. Remember, you must speak of something being **done**, but must not show that it was done **to** any body, **or to** any thing.

When the verb shows that something has been done to the subject of the sentence, instead of being done **by** him, it is called a **Passive Verb.** Thus, in the sentence—

"The dog was **flogged** by Thomas,"

dog is the subject of the sentence, and Thomas is the object; and, you see, it was the **dog** that got the flogging; **he** did nothing—he was **only flogged**—so here the verb is said to be in the passive voice.

EXAMPLES OF PASSIVE VERBS.

Exercise 57.

Copy the following sentences, and draw a line under the passive verbs:—

That bridge was built by Rennie.
The child has been frightened.
How were you hurt?
Is your sum finished?
In the corn-fields poor Mary is seen.
America was discovered by Columbus.

The boys are taught by their master.

That purse was lost by William.

The parcel was sent by papa.

The ship was wrecked in the storm.

That is drawn by Edgar.

My box was packed by mamma.

EXERCISE 58.

Write twelve sentences, each containing a passive verb. Remember, you must let your verb show that the subject of the sentence has been **acted upon**—that is, that something has been done to it.

MOOD.

"Mood," or "mode," means the manner in which the verb expresses an action; for, you know, a verb may tell that something has been done, or it may order something to be done. The easiest way for you to learn the moods will be to copy this lesson, and call it

Exercise (or Lesson) 59.

Verbs have five moods.

1. The **Indicative Mood.**

The indicative mood simply indicates, or tells of something being done—as, "Mary **sings.**"

2. The **Imperative Mood.**

The imperative mood orders or entreats that something may be done—as, "Mary, **sing,**" or, "Mary, **do** sing."

3. The **Conditional Mood.**

As you will see by its name, this mood shows that a condition is made—as, "**If** Mary **sing,** I shall be glad."

4. The **Potential Mood.**

The potential mood shows power, or gives permission to do something—as, "Mary **may** sing," or, "Mary **can** sing."

5. The **Infinitive Mood.**

This mood merely tells of something being done; as, "To sing."

EXERCISE 60.

Give another example of each of the moods.

Besides showing the manner, or mood, in which the verb is used, we must point out the time at which the action takes place. The time, then, is called the

TENSE.

There are three principal tenses—namely, the **present** tense, the **past** tense, and the **future** tense—and of course you can understand that these mean what you **are doing**, what you **have done**, and what you are **going to do.** As

Present.	*Past.*	*Future.*
I walk.	I walked.	I shall walk.

Now, this is called the *imperfect* form, for, you

observe, neither walk, walked, or shall walk, show that the act is **finished.** The *perfect* form is as follows :—

Present.	*Past.*	*Future.*
I have walked.	I had walked.	I shall have walked.

Thus in the present perfect tense you show that you have **finished** your walk ; in the perfect past you show that you **had finished** your walk **at a certain time,** or *before you did something else ;* and in the perfect future you say that you **will have finished** your walk *before something else occurs.* I will try to make you understand this. Supposing you to meet a boy at the door of your school. He has ridden to school, although he lives only close by, so you say to him—

"I **have walked** to school this morning, and **before** starting, I **had walked** in the garden. I **shall walk** in the playground, and **shall have walked** home before papa comes from the city."

Exercise 61.

Write down the present, past, and future tenses of three verbs, in the imperfect and perfect form.

I will put off teaching you any more about four of the moods until you are a little older, so will only, at present, speak of the Indicative, and will show you how the verb is altered according to the **person** acting, or the **time** at which the action is done.

Indicative Mood.

Present Imperfect Tense.

	Singular.	*Plural.*
1st person	I play	We play.
2nd person	Thou playest	You (or Ye) play
3rd person	He (She or It) plays	They play

Present Perfect Tense.

	Singular.	*Plural.*
1st person	I have played	We have played
2nd person	Thou hast played	You have played
3rd person	He has played	They have played

Past Imperfect Tense.

	Singular.	*Plural.*
1st person	I played	We played
2nd person	Thou didst play	You played
3rd person	He played	They played

Past Perfect Tense.

	Singular.	*Plural.*
1st person	I had played	We had played
2nd person	Thou hadst played	You had played
3rd person	He had played	They had played

Future Imperfect Tense.

	Singular.	*Plural.*
1st person	I shall play	We shall play
2nd person	Thou shalt (or wilt) play	You shall play
3rd person	He shall (or will) play	They shall play

Future Perfect Tense.

	Singular.
1st person	I shall have played
2nd person	Thou shalt (or wilt) have played
3rd person	He shall (or will) have played
	Plural.
1st person	We shall (or will) have played
2nd person	You shall (or will) have played
3rd person	They shall (or will) have played

When we follow up a verb through all its moods and tenses we are said to **con-ju-gate** it.

EXERCISE (OR LESSON) 62.

Copy and learn the present imperfect and perfect tenses.

Exercise (or Lesson) 63.

Copy and learn the past imperfect and perfect tenses.

Exercise (or Lesson) 64.

Copy and learn the future imperfect and perfect tenses.

You will see that to alter the present tense of the verb "play" into the past tense I added **ed**, and so turned the word "play" into **played**.

Now, all verbs which can be turned from the present to the past tense by adding **d** or **ed**, are called **regular**. The following are some of the

Regular Verbs.

Present.	*Past.*	*Present.*	*Past.*
Belong	Belonged	Follow	Followed
Discharge	Discharged	Join	Joined
Fear	Feared	Live	Lived
Look	Looked	Help	Helped
Love	Loved	Open	Opened
Please	Pleased	Praise	Praised
Use	Used	Return	Returned

EXERCISE 65.

Copy the regular verbs on the last page, and draw a line under the letters which have been added to turn the present into the past.

EXERCISE 66.

Copy these regular verbs, and add the past tense in the other column.

Present.	*Past.*	*Present.*	*Past.*
Work	———	Grant	———
Plant	———	Light	———
Clean	———	Step	———
Dance	———	Jump	———
Wish	———	Paint	———

EXERCISE 67.

Copy these regular verbs, and add the present tense to them.

Present.	*Past.*	*Present.*	*Past.*
———	Grazed	———	Sawed
———	Invited	———	Glued
———	Hoped	———	Fixed
———	Mended	———	Scraped
———	Framed	———	Lifted

EXERCISE 68.

Write down ten more regular verbs, in the past and present tenses.

All verbs which do not form their past tense by adding **d** or **ed** to the present tense, are called Irregular. The following are some of the

IRREGULAR VERBS.

EXERCISE AND LESSON 69.

Copy and learn the following irregular verbs :—

Present.	*Past.*	*Present.*	*Past.*
Arise	Arose	Write	Wrote
See	Saw	Break	Broke
Cut	Cut	Do	Did
Am	Was	Have	Had
Go	Went	Shall	Should
Begin	Began	Can	Could
Speak	Spoke	Buy	Bought
Choose	Chose	Bite	Bit
Build	Built	Creep	Crept
Fall	Fell	Dwell	Dwelt
Fight	Fought	Leave	Left
Hold	Held	Kneel	Knelt

Exercise 70.

Copy the following irregular verbs, and add the past tense in the opposite column :—

Present.	*Past.*	*Present.*	*Past.*
Steal	———	Leave	———
Come	———	Get	———
Eat	———	Grow	———
Feel	———	Hit	———
Flee	———	Lose	———
Give	———	Read	———
Grind	———	Seek	———
Hear	———	Sell	———
Hide	———	Shake	———
Kneel	———	Sing	———
Know	———	Sow	———

Exercise 71.

Copy the following irregular verbs, which are in the past tense, and add the present tense in the opposite column :—

Present.	*Past.*	*Present.*	*Past.*
———	Froze	———	Meant
———	Hurt	———	Put
———	Lent	———	Shone
———	Took	———	Won
———	Wove	———	Tore
———	Thought	———	Trod
———	Stuck	———	Stung
———	Rang	———	Paid
———	Laid	———	Bled
———	Caught	———	Ate
———	Dealt	———	Rose
———	Bound	———	Spun

EXERCISE 72.

Read the following little tale. Write down all the verbs in it. Place them in two columns, the regular verbs in one, and the irregular in the other. To any that are in the past add the present, and to such as are in the present add the past.

WHY THE BEAR HAS A STUMPY TAIL.

One day a bear met a fox, who came slinking along with a string of fish, which of course he had stolen.

"Where did you get these?" asked the bear.

"Oh, my lord Bruin," said the fox, "I have been out fishing, and caught them."

So the bear had a mind to learn to fish, too; and bade the fox tell him how to set about it.

"Oh," answered the cunning gentleman, "it is an easy craft for you, and soon learned. You have only to go upon the ice, cut a hole, and stick your tail into it; and then you must go on holding it there as long as you can. You must not mind if your tail smarts a little, that is when the fish bite. The longer you hold it in, the more fish you will get, and then all at once pull it out with a cross pull, sideways, and with a strong pull, too."

So the bear did as the fox had said, and held his tail a long, long time down the hole till it was frozen fast. Then he pulled it out with a cross pull, *and, lo! it snapped off short.* This is why the bear goes about with a stumpy tail to this day.

I think I must now leave off teaching you about verbs themselves, so that I may tell you what words are used together with verbs, to show whether the act has been done well or ill.

You will remember that I told you that adjectives point out the quality of **nouns,** so that, in the sentence, "What beautiful writing," the adjective *beautiful* tells us what **sort of writing** it is; but if I say, "John writes **beautifully,**" then the word **beautifully** tells us **how** John **writes**; it does not tell us about the writing, but how **John writes.**

¶ Words which are used to show **how** any thing

is, how it is done, **when** it was done, or **where** it was done, are called

ADVERBS.

EXERCISE 73.

Copy and learn the above rule, commencing at the mark ¶, then copy the following examples of the uses of adverbs :—

The birds sing **sweetly.**

We shall have a holiday **to-morrow.**

He went **there.**

The child dances **prettily.**

EXERCISE 74. (*Examples Continued.*)

The sun shines **brightly.**

The boy draws **well.**

The dog was **cruelly** treated.

We lived **happily.**

We played **merrily.**

He ran **quickly.**

I walked **slowly.**

He calls **daily.**

You will observe that several of the adverbs which end in **ly**, are formed from adjectives. Thus, in the sentence, "The bird sings sweetly," if you had said, "The bird sings a **sweet** song," the word "sweet" would have been an adjective, but as you want to show **how the bird sings**, you add **ly** to the adjective, and then the word "sweetly" is an adverb.

Again, in the sentence, "I walked slowly," if you had said, "I took a slow walk," "slow" would have been an adjective; but as you wish to tell **how** you **walked**, you add **ly** to the adjective slow, and **slowly** becomes an adverb.

Exercise and Lesson 75.

Copy **and learn** the following:—

There are six kinds of adverbs.

1. Adverbs of **time**, which point out **when** anything has been done; as, **to-day, yesterday, to-morrow, now.**

2. Adverbs of **place**, which tell **where** the action takes place; as, **here, there, afar, near, backward, forward.**

3. Adverbs of **quantity.** These point out **how often** an act has taken place, or **how much** has been done; as, **much, little, enough, half, once, twice,** &c.

Exercise and Lesson 76.

4. Adverbs of **manner,** which tell **how** anything has been done; as, **well, ill, quietly, clearly,** &c.

5. Adverbs of **affirmation,** which affirm, that is, say **yes** to, or confirm an act; as, **yes, yea, aye.**

6. Adverbs of **negation,** which give denial; as, **no, not, nay, not at all.**

Exercise 77.

Copy the following, in which you will see how these adverbs are used:—

"I met William, **yesterday.** I asked him to come **here.** I asked him **twice.** I spoke **kindly** to him. He said, **yes**; but he did **not** come."

Now, adverbs may always be known by their answering questions, such as How? how much? when? or where? Thus:—

Time.—**When** did you meet William? **Yesterday.**

Place.—**Where** (or to what place) did you ask him to come? **Here.**

Quantity.—How often (or how much) had you asked him? **Twice.**

Manner.—How did you speak to him? **Kindly.**

Affirmation.—What did he say as to coming? **Yes.**

Negation.—Did he come? He did **not.**

Exercise 78.

Write six sentences, each containing an adverb. Separate the adverbs, and state of which kind they are

Exercise or Lesson 79.

Copy and learn the following:—

Adverbs are also used to increase or lessen the quality expressed by an adjective.

If you say, "A nice cake," "nice" is an adjective; but if you have found the cake full of currants, candied peel, and all sorts of good things, you will say it was a **very** nice cake; so here, you see, the adverb **very** has made the cake better than the adjective said it was.

Exercise 80.

Copy the following examples of adverbs used with adjectives.

A **very** *high* tower.

A **strictly** *honest* man.

An **ex-ceed-ing-ly** *fine* day.

A **rather** *pretty* dog.

An **almost** *empty* cup.

Exercise 81.

Write six more examples of adverbs used together with adjectives.

Exercise 82.

Copy and learn the following:—

An adverb is sometimes used to add to, or take from, the strength of another adverb.

EXAMPLES:

It is **very well** done.
She was **only poorly** clad.
He comes **tol-er-a-bly often.**
She sings **pretty well.**

Write two more sentences, using one adverb to strengthen or weaken the meaning of another in each sentence.

EXERCISE 83.

Copy the following sentences. Draw **two** lines under the **adverbs,** and **one** line under the **adjectives.**

John rides less awkwardly than Henry.
Sarah is a very good girl.
The book is well written.
The field is thickly covered with grass.
He left early.
I have seen that child before.

Exercise 84.

Copy and sort out from the following sentences the adverbs of time, place, manner, and quantity.

I always do my work.
I often see Richard.
I shall meet him to-night.
He cried aloud.
She will be there to-morrow.
I shall soon know my lesson perfectly.
He was very well paid.
They played too noisily.

Exercise 85.

Complete the following sentences by adverbs.

The dog barks ——	The child plays ————
It rains ————	It is —— painted.
John runs ————	The engine moves ————
How —— the boy behaved.	How —— the sun shines.
The army fought —	The oven is —— large.
The book is—bound.	The child speaks ———

EXERCISE 86.

Copy the following, which are a few of the adverbs often used:—

Aboard	Aloof	Away	Else
About	Already	Backward	Enough
Afar	Always	Before	Ere
Afloat	Amiss	Behind	Even
Afterward	Apart	Daily	Ever
Again	As	Doubly	Far
Aground	Ashore	Doubtless	Fast
Alike	Aside	Down	First
Almost	Asleep	Early	Forth
Alone	Asunder	Easily	Forward

EXERCISE 87.

List of Adverbs—Continued.

Gratis	Here	Indeed	More
Gravely	Hither	Least	Most
Greatly	How	Less	Much
Happily	However	Likewise	Name
Hence	Ill	Little	Namely

Never	Outward	Somewhat	Very
No	Partly	Soon	Well
Not	Perhaps	Still	Whence
Now	Quite	Then	Where
Off	Rather	Thence	While
Oft	Scarcely	Thither	Whilst
Often	Seldom	Thus	Whither
Once	Since	To-day	Why
Only	So	Together	Yes
Out	Sometimes	Upwards	Yet

PREPOSITIONS.

EXERCISE 88.

Copy and learn—

Prepositions show the relation between different words or ideas.

EXAMPLES:

The man is **in** the house.

John is **at** school.

He climbs **up** a ladder.
He got **under** cover.
I sat **near** my mother.
I was **with** my brother.
It was **during** the day.
He fell **between** the desks.

Exercise 89.

Copy the following principal prepositions :—

About	Along	At	Beside
Above	Amid	Athwart	Between
According to	Amidst	Before	Betwixt
Across	Among	Behind	Beyond
After	Amongst	Below	By
Against	Around	Beneath	Concerning

Exercise 90.

List of Prepositions—Continued.

Down	For	Instead of	Nigh
During	From	Into	Of
Except	In	Near	On

Out of	Save	Touching	Up
Over	Since	Towards	Upon
Regarding	Through	Under	With
Respecting	Throughout	Underneath	Within
Round	To	Unto	Without

EXERCISE 91.

Copy the following examples of prepositions:—

He went **from** London **to** York.

They support themselves **by** work.

He came **on** horseback.

He stood **before** the fire.

A pound **of** cherries.

I went **with** him.

EXERCISE 92.

The Uses of Prepositions—Continued.

The Thames is **between** the City and Southwark.

The sun moves **round** the earth.

The dog ran **across** the field.

I shall be there **within** an hour.

I wish to see you **concerning** the matter.

It has happened **since** I left.

Sometimes we do not really **use** a preposition, but we **mean** one. When a word is really used we say it is **expressed**; when we do not use it, but still write the sentence as if it were really there, the word is said to be **understood.** Thus, in the following sentence,

"Bring me those marbles,"

the preposition **to** is **understood,** for the sentence really means "bring **to** me those marbles," that is, "bring those marbles **to** me."

Exercise 93.

Copy the following examples; the preposition printed in small letters and between brackets, [ ], would be understood, not written.

Lend [to] me your pen-knife.

Make [for] me a boat like yours.

Fetch [to] me my stick.

Write [to] me a letter.

Exercise 94.

Copy the following sentences, and put in the prepositions which are **understood.**

He told me what had happened.

Send me a box of toys.

Cut me some flowers.

He made me a box.

Exercise 95.

Write four sentences in which the prepositions are **understood,** but not expressed.

Now, before we travel any further on this road to grammar, let us pause and see if you remember what you have learnt, and the following little poem will help us to do this :—

WHAT CLOTHES ARE MADE OF.

1.

Come here to papa, and I'll tell you, my boy,
For I think you would never have guessed,
How many poor animals we must employ,
Before little Charles can be dressed.

2.

The pretty sheep gives you the wool from his side
 To make you a jacket to use;
And the ox or the horse must be stripped of its hide
 To give you a couple of shoes.

Exercise 96.

Copy these two verses, then pick out all the articles, nouns, adjectives, pronouns, verbs, adverbs, and prepositions. Place the different sorts of words in separate columns. There are some of the words, such as "and," which you have not learnt about yet, but we shall go on again presently, and then you will soon be able to sort out all the words that are used.

Now we will finish our poem.

3.

And then the grey rabbit next gives you his share,
 He helps to provide you a hat;
For this is oft made of his delicate hair,
 And so you may thank him for that.

4.

And many poor animals suffer besides,
  And each of them gives us a share;
Pull off their warm clothing, or give us their hides,
  That we may have plenty to wear.

5.

Then, as the poor creatures are suffered to give
  So much for the comfort of man,
I think 'tis but right that as long as they live
  We should do for **them** all that we can.

Exercise 97.

Copy these three verses, and sort out the words as you did in the last exercise. When we sort out words, and tell all about their being verbs or nouns, or any other kind of word, and state all we know about their mood, their tense, their person, number, gender, case, we are said to be **parsing** the sentence. To "parse" a sentence, then, means to sort out the different kinds of words, and explain all about them.

In the first verse of this poem you will see the word I'll: this means **I will.** The w and i of the word **will** are left out, and an apostrophe is put above their place instead of them. In the fourth verse, too, there is the word '*tis*, which means **it** is.

CONJUNCTIONS.

Conjunctions are used to join words or sentences together; as,

"You **and** I."

Write down this; but when I say write it down, I do not mean that you are only just to put it down in your exercise book, but that you are to "write it in the tablet of **your memory,**" so that you may not only copy it, but **know** it.

"Oh!" you will say, "what a nice short lesson I am to have for to-morrow." Do not make too sure of that, my child, for I am going to ask you to copy and learn some of the following conjunctions; so you see you are not to get off quite so easily as you thought.

Exercise 98.

List of Conjunctions most frequently used.

Also	Furthermore	Save
And	Hence	Since
As	However	Than
Because	If	That
Besides	Lest	Then
But	Likewise	Therefore
Either	Moreover	Though
Else	Neither	Too
Ever	Nevertheless	Unless
Except	Nor	Whereas
For	Notwithstanding	Wherefore
Further	Or	Yet

Exercise 99.

Examples of the Use of Conjunctions.

John **and** Peter are good boys.

Your house is larger **than** ours.

He can **neither** read **nor** write.

They may go **or** stay.

He will come, **for** he promised.

I will take **either** one **or** the other.

Exercise 100.

Examples of the Use of Conjunctions—Continued.

I will forgive him **if** he is sorry.

Walk carefully **lest** you fall.

You will not succeed **unless** you work.

I cannot spare much, **but** will give a trifle.

I will go **since** you wish it.

He was careless, **therefore** he failed.

Exercise 101.

Write six sentences, each containing one conjunction or more.

Exercise 102.

Write six sentences, using one of the following conjunctions in each :—

Nevertheless	Because
However	Yet
Likewise	Save

INTERJECTIONS.

EXERCISE 103.

Copy and learn the following :—

Interjections are used to express sorrow, joy, pain surprise, or other feeling.

SORROW.—"**Alas**! he fell."

JOY.—"**Hurrah**! we have won."

PAIN.—"**Oh**! how I suffer."

SURPRISE.—"**Indeed**! is it so?"

CONTEMPT.—"**Pshaw**! what nonsense."

SATISFACTION.—"**Bravo**! **bravo**! well done."

EXERCISE 104.

Write six sentences in which interjections are used.

CAPITAL LETTERS.

The first word of a new sentence, either at the beginning of what you are writing or after a full stop, must begin with a capital. Examples :—

"I was the third of the boys. Two of our sisters were older than any of us. I loved them, and they all loved me. Not that we ever talked about that. I knew it, and felt it."

All proper names must begin with capitals; as, "John, Sarah, London."

The pronoun I and the interjection Oh must be written in capitals; as, "Oh! how glad I am."

Adjectives which are formed from proper nouns must begin with capitals; as, "Englishmen are brave," "the French language."

The names of the months of the year, the days of the week, and the holidays must begin with capitals; as, "The Christmas holidays begin on Tuesday, the 22nd of December, and end on Monday, the 14th of January."

We must begin to write the name of any book, or the title of any person, with a capital; as, "Cassell's Right Lines," "Captain Williams."

The names of all great events mentioned in

history, as "the Reformation," "tho Restoration," "the Rebellion of 1715," must begin with capitals.

The first letter of every line of poetry must be a capital.

QUESTIONS FOR ORAL EXAMINATION.

Answer only the question you are asked. Use as few words as possible.

1. What are nouns?
2. Look about you, and tell me some nouns.
3. Tell me the nouns in this sentence:—"I went into the garden, and fetched some apples in a basket."
4. How many letters are there in the English language?
5. What are the names of the two sorts into which letters are divided?
6. How many vowels are there? Repeat them.
7. How many consonants are there?
8. What is the difference between vowels and consonants?
9. What is meant by singular, and what by plural? Tell me some nouns of the singular and some of the plural number.

10. How would you turn the following singular nouns into the plural number?—Book, cat, dog, pen, nut, box, church, watch.
11. How would you form the plural of such words as negro, hero, knife, leaf, calf, loaf, fly, cherry, lady, goose, mouth, tooth, penny, foot?
12. What is meant by gender?
13. Tell me the names of the genders, and explain their meaning.
14. Tell me the feminine gender of boy, man, father, husband, and of boar, dog, gander, son.
15. Give me the masculine of cow. aunt, mare, niece, lady.
16. Tell me the feminine genders of giant, prophet, priest, and tiger.
17. Look around the room, and tell me some nouns of the neuter gender.
18. Of what gender are the following nouns?—Animals, people, children, friends, parents.
19. What is meant by nominative case, what by possessive, and what by objective?

20. Give me a sentence in which a noun is in the nominative case, one in which it is in the possessive, and another in which it is in the objective.

21. What is an "apostrophe," and how is it used?

22. What is meant by common and proper nouns? Tell me some of each.

23. What are "articles," and how many are there of them?

24. Which is the definite and which the indefinite article? Why are they called by these names?

25. When do we change the article "**a**" into **an**? Tell me some words with which we should use **a**, and some others before which we should place **an**.

26. What are "adjectives?"

27. Give me some sentences, to show the use of adjectives.

28. What is meant by the "three degrees of comparison?"

29. Compare the following adjectives:—Good, great, pretty, sweet, dark, beautiful, fortunate.
30. Form adjectives from the following nouns:—India, China, Rome, Africa.
31. Tell me the adjectives which have exactly the opposite meaning to the following:—Good, coarse, right, long, clean, quick.
32. What are pronouns?
33. Give me a sentence showing how a pronoun is used.
34. Tell me the names of the different kinds of pronouns.
35. What is meant by first, second, and third person?
36. Tell me the first, second, and third persons in the singular and plural.
37. Tell me the nominative, possessive, and objective cases of the first person singular.
38. Give me the nominative, possessive, and objective of the second person plural.
39. Which are the relative pronouns, and what is their use?

40. Which of the relative pronouns is used to persons, which to animals or things, and which may be used to either?

41. Which are the possessive pronouns? Give me a sentence showing how they are used.

42. What are the in-ter-rog-a-tive pronouns? Give me a sentence in which one is used.

43. What are verbs?

44. Give me a sentence to show how verbs are used.

45. What is meant by transitive and what by intransitive verbs?

46. Give me a sentence in which a transitive verb is used.

47. Give me another sentence, using an intransitive verb.

48. What is meant by a passive verb?

49. Give me a sentence in which a passive verb is used.

50. What is meant by mood?

51. Name the principal moods.

52. Give an example of each of the following moods—the indicative, the imperative.

53. Give an example of each of the following verbs—the conditional, the potential, the infinitive.

54. What is meant by tense?

55. Mention the principal tenses.

56. Give an example of the imperfect and perfect form of each tense.

57. Repeat the present imperfect tense of the verb "walk."

58. Tell me the present perfect tense of the same verb.

59. Repeat the imperfect and perfect tenses of the verb "work."

60. Tell me the imperfect and perfect future tenses of the verb "mend."

61. What is the difference between regular and irregular verbs?

62. Give an example of each.

63. Tell me the past tense of each of the following verbs—dance, wish, saw, arise, write, kneel, creep, buy, come.

64. Which of these are regular and which irregular verbs?

65. The following verbs are in the past tense, tell me the present of each:—Froze, lent, rang, caught, ate, bled, trod.

66. What are adverbs?

67. How would you know if a word is an adverb or an adjective?

68. In which of the following sentences do you find an adjective, and in which an adverb?

 I have a bright penny.

 The sun shines brightly.

69. How many kinds of adverbs are generally used?

70. What is shown by adverbs of time? Give me a sentence in which one is used.

71. Give an example of an adverb of place.

72. Give me a sentence in which an adverb of quantity is used

73. How are adverbs of manner used? Give an example.

74. What is meant by an adverb of affirmation? Give a sentence in which one is used.

75. Show the use of adverbs of negation.

76. Give an example in which an adverb is used together with an adjective.

77. Give me a sentence in which an adverb is used to strengthen or weaken another.

78. "I rise early, and often take a walk. Sometimes I gather flowers, which my mamma likes very much." Tell me the adverbs in these sentences.

79. Tell me six adverbs of quantity.

80. Tell me six adverbs of time.

81. Tell me six adverbs of place.

82. Give six adverbs of manner.

83. What are prepositions?

84. Give a sentence in which a preposition is used.

85. "I ran up the ladder quickly. I came down slowly." Which are prepositions and which are adverbs in these sentences?

86. Tell me six prepositions.

87. What is meant by **expressed** or **understood?**

88. Give me a sentence in which a preposition is expressed.

89. Give another in which the preposition is **understood.**

90. What prepositions are understood in the following sentences? "Gather me some flowers." "Please give me a penny."

91. What is meant by parsing?

92. Parse the following sentences:

    I love my sister.

    He gave me a large cake.

    John wrote his exercise nicely.

93. What are conjunctions?

94. Give me three sentences in which conjunctions are used.

95. Tell me six conjunctions.

96. The word **save** is sometimes a verb and sometimes a conjunction. Give me an example of its being used first as one, then as the other.

97. What are interjections?

98. Give examples of interjections used to express sorrow, joy, pain, surprise, contempt, satisfaction.

99. In writing sentences, which words should always have capital letters?

100. What sort of nouns, what pronoun, and what interjection should always have capitals?

101. What adjectives should begin with capitals?

102. In what other cases should capitals be used?

SELECTIONS

FROM

CASSELL, PETTER, AND GALPIN'S

CATALOGUE,

COMPRISING

CHILDREN'S BOOKS

AND

ILLUSTRATED GIFT BOOKS

SUITABLE FOR

PRIZES, REWARDS AND GIFTS.

CASSELL, PETTER, AND GALPIN,

LONDON AND NEW YORK.

CHILDREN'S LIBRARY.—*Continued.*

Crocker the Clown: A Tale for Boys. By B. CLARKE. Editor of "Kind Words." Handsomely Illustrated. Cloth, gilt, 3s. 6d.

King Gab's Story Bag; and the Wondrous Tales it contained. By HERACLITUS GREY. With Illustrations by WALTER CRANE. Cloth, gilt, 3s. 6d.

Hours of Sunshine: A Series of Poems for Children. By MATTHIAS BARR, Author of "Little Willie," &c. With 16 Coloured Plates from Designs by OSCAR PLETSCH. 3s. 6d.

Playing Trades. By HERACLITUS GREY, Author of "King Gab," &c. With 16 Coloured Plates, from Designs by J. BARFOOT. Cloth, gilt, 3s. 6d.

ONE SYLLABLE SERIES.

Æsop's Fables, in Words of One Syllable. With Illustrations printed in Colours by KRONHEIM. Handsomely bound in cloth, gilt, 3s. 6d.

Sandford and Merton, in Words of One Syllable. With Illustrations printed in Colours by KRONHEIM. Handsomely bound in cloth, gilt, 3s. 6d.

Reynard the Fox; the Rare Romance of, and the Shifts of his Son Reynardine. In Words of One Syllable. By SAMUEL PHILLIPS DAY. With Coloured Illustrations by KRONHEIM, from Designs by ERNEST GRISET. 3s. 6d.

The Pilgrim's Progress. In Words of One Syllable. By S. PHILLIPS DAY. With Coloured Illustrations by KRONHEIM. 3s. 6d.

The Swiss Family Robinson. In Words of One Syllable. By the Author of "The Boy's First Reader." Coloured Illustrations from Designs by GRISET, CRANE, &c. 3s. 6d.

Evenings at Home. In Words of One Syllable. By the Author of "The Children's Album." Coloured Illustrations from Designs by DOWNARD, BAYES, &c. 3s. 6d.

PRIZE BOOK SERIES.

Handsomely bound in extra cloth, gilt, gilt edges.

UNIFORM IN SIZE AND PRICE.

Will Adams: the Adventures of the First Englishman in Japan. By WILLIAM DALTON. 3s. 6d.

Working Women of this Century: the Lesson of their Lives. By CLARA LUCAS BALFOUR. 3s. 6d.

Famous Regiments of the British Army. By WILLIAM H. DAVENPORT. 3s. 6d.

The Angel of the Iceberg, and other Stories. By JOHN TODD, D.D. (New Edition.) 3s. 6d.

The Book of Drawing-room Plays and Evening Amusements. A Comprehensive Manual of Indoor Recreation, including all kinds of Acting Charades, &c. Illustrated by DU MAURIER and CORBOULD. 3s. 6d.

TWO SHILLING SERIES

OF NEW AND ORIGINAL WORKS.

Bound in best cloth, gilt edges, with Coloured Illustrations.

Beatrice Langton; or, the Spirit of Obedience. 2s.

New Stories and Old Legends. By Mrs. T. K. HERVEY. With Illustrations printed in Colours. Cloth, gilt, 2s.

Owen Carstone: a Story of School Life. With Illustrations printed in Colours. Cloth, gilt, 2s.

The Boy who Wondered. By the Author of "Ups and Downs in an Old Maid's Life." 2s.

The Little Orphan. Coloured Illustrations by KRONHEIM. Cloth, lettered, 2s.

The Story of Arthur Hunter and his First Shilling. 2s.

The Story of the Hamiltons. With Illustrations printed in Colours. Cloth, gilt, 2s.

The Hillside Farm. Cloth, gilt, 2s.

EIGHTEENPENNY SERIES

OF NEW AND ORIGINAL WORKS.

Bound in best cloth, gilt edges, with Four Coloured Plates by KRONHEIM *in each Book.*

The Holidays at Llandudno.

The Hop Garden: A Story of Town and Country Life.

Algy's Lesson. By S. E. DE MORGAN.

Ashfield Farm; or, Ellen and Robert's First Journey from Home.

Grandmamma's Spectacles. By the Author of "A Trap to Catch a Sunbeam."

Hid in a Cave; or, the Lost Child.

Little Fables for Little Folks.

Flora Selwyn: A Story for Girls.

CASSELL'S

SHILLING STORY BOOKS.

Little Lizzie. By MARY GILLIES. And other Tales. 1s.

Luke Barnicott. By WILLIAM HOWITT. And other Tales. 1s.

My First Cruise. By W. H. KINGSTON. And other Tales. 1s.

The Boat Club. By OLIVER OPTIC. And other Tales. 1s.

The Delft Jug. By SILVERPEN. And other Tales. 1s.

The Elchester College Boys. By Mrs. HENRY WOOD. And other Tales. 1s.

The Little Peacemaker. By MARY HOWITT. And other Tales. 1s.

The Secret Society. By Mrs. DE MORGAN. And other Tales. 1s.

SHILLING TOY BOOKS.

In demy 4to, stiff covers. With full-page Illustrations printed in Colours by KRONHEIM.

1. **How Cock Sparrow Spent his Christmas.**
2. **The Adventures of Robinson Crusoe.**
3. **Queer Creatures, Drawn by One of Themselves.**
4. **Æsop's Fables.** (21 Plates.)

PICTURE-TEACHING SERIES.

Picture Natural History. A Series of Plates numbering upwards of 700, in which the Animal, Vegetable, and Mineral Kingdoms are classified in Families. With Descriptive Letterpress. Edited by the Rev. C. BOUTELL, M.A. 4to, cloth, lettered, 5s.

Picture Teaching for Young and Old: A Series of Object Lessons Progressively Arranged, so as to teach the meaning of every term employed. With more than 200 Illustrations, 4to, cloth, lettered, 5s.

THE

BELLE SAUVAGE LIBRARY.

A SERIES OF VOLUMES FOR FAMILY AND HOME READING.

Handsomely bound in bevelled boards, red edges, price 3s. 6d. *per volume.*

1. **Pulpit Table Talk.** Containing Remarks and Anecdotes on Preachers and Preaching. By EDWIN B. RAMSAY, M.A., LL.D., F.R.S.E., Dean of Edinburgh.
2. **The Search for the Gral.** By JULIA GODDARD, Author of "Joyce Dormer's Story," "Adriana," &c. &c.
3. **Sermons for Boys.** By the Rev. ALFRED BARRY, D.D., Principal of King's College, London, late Head Master of Cheltenham Grammar School.
4. **The Life of Bernard Palissy, of Saintes.** By HENRY MORLEY, Professor of English Literature in University College, London.
5. **The Young Man in the Battle of Life.** By the Rev. Dr. LANDELS, Author of "Woman: her Sphere," &c.

ILLUSTRATED GIFT BOOKS.

The Child's Bible. Large Print; Large Pictures. Being a Selection from the Holy Bible in the words of the Authorised Version, with large full-page Illustrations, especially designed for Children by the best Artists of the day. Cloth, elegant, gilt edges, £1 1s.; flexible leather binding, hand-tooled, gilt edges, £1 10s.; best morocco, elegant, £2 2s.

Æsop's Fables. A new and carefully revised Version of these Fables. By J. B. RUNDELL. Profusely Illustrated with Original Designs by ERNEST GRISET. Cloth, gilt, gilt edges, 21s.

Fairy Realm. A Collection of the Favourite Old Tales. Illustrated by GUSTAVE DORÉ, and Told in Verse by TOM HOOD. Imperial 4to, £1 1s.

The Adventures of Munchausen. Illustrated by GUSTAVE DORÉ. 4to, cloth, 10s. 6d.

Robinson Crusoe. New Royal 8vo Edition, beautifully illustrated throughout. Plain cloth, 5s.; full gilt, cloth, gilt edges, 6s. 6d.

Swiss Family Robinson. 100 Illustrations by GRISET, YAN D'ARGENT, &c., with Coloured Frontispiece. Cloth, plain, 5s.; cloth, extra gilt, gilt edges, 6s. 6d.

The World of Wonders: A Record of Things Wonderful in Nature, Science, and Art. Cloth, plain, 7s. 6d.; full gilt cloth, gilt edges, 10s. 6d.

Foxe's Book of Martyrs. Edited by the Rev. W. BRAMLEY-MOORE, M.A. Illustrated with full-page Designs by the best Artists. Imperial 8vo, plain cloth, 12s.; full gilt cloth, gilt edges, 15s.

ILLUSTRATED GIFT BOOKS.—*Continued.*

THE ILLUSTRATED LIBRARY. Plain cloth, 7s. 6d.; full gilt cloth, gilt edges, 10s. 6d.; morocco antique, 21s. each.

Cassell's Book of Sacred Poems. Illustrated. Edited by the Rev. R. H. BAYNES, M.A., Editor of "Lyra Anglicana."

Cassell's Illustrated Bunyan. The PILGRIM'S PROGRESS. Illustrated throughout.

Cassell's Illustrated Bunyan. The HOLY WAR. Illustrated throughout.

Cassell's Illustrated Gulliver. GULLIVER'S TRAVELS. By DEAN SWIFT. Profusely illustrated throughout by MORTEN.

Cassell's Illustrated Robinson Crusoe. Beautifully illustrated throughout.

Cassell's Illustrated Readings. Conducted by TOM HOOD. In Two Vols., each complete in itself.

Goldsmith's Works. The VICAR of WAKEFIELD and POEMS. Illustrated throughout.

Little Songs for Me to Sing. Illustrated by J. E. MILLAIS, R.A.; with Music composed expressly for the work by HENRY LESLIE. Square crown 8vo (*Dedicated by express permission to Her Royal Highness the* PRINCESS OF WALES), 6s.

Bright Thoughts for the Little Ones. Twenty-seven Original Drawings by PROCTER. With Prose and Verse by GRANDMAMMA. Cloth, lettered, gilt edges, 7s. 6d.

The Child's Garland of Little Poems; Rhymes for Little People. With Exquisite Illustrative Borders by Giacomelli. Square 8vo, cloth, gilt, 7s. 6d.

Old Friends and New Faces. Demy 4to, cloth, elegantly gilt, with Twenty-four full-page Illustrations, beautifully printed by KRONHEIM, 5s.

The Natural History of the Three Kingdoms. With Coloured Plates, and Text in English, French, and German. Oblong 4to, coloured boards, 3s. 6d.